Instant Moodle Quiz Module How-to

Create Moodle quizzes to enhance learning using practical, hands-on recipes

Joan Coy

BIRMINGHAM - MUMBAI

Instant Moodle Quiz Module How-to

First published: January 2013

Production Reference: 1170113

Published by Packt Publishing Ltd.
Livery Place
35 Livery Street
Birmingham B3 2PB, UK.

ISBN 978-1-84951-988-5

www.packtpub.com

Credits

Author
Joan Coy

Reviewers
Rafael Reyna Camones

David Le Blanc

Acquisition Editor
Joanna Finchen

Commissioning Editor
Meeta Rajani

Technical Editor
Prasad Dalvi

Project Coordinator
Shraddha Bagadia

Proofreader
Katherine Tarr

Production Coordinator
Melwyn D'sa

Cover Work
Melwyn D'sa

Cover Image
Conidon Miranda

About the Author

Joan Coy has taught High School Math and Science in Canada for over 30 years. She is currently the Principal of PAVE, a Grade 4 to 12 online school (which is using Moodle as the LMS). Being a Moodle Certified Teacher, she administers on the PAVE site, and has taught online Moodle training courses with Open2Know. Joan chairs an Alberta wide educator group for the purpose of sharing Moodle courses and best practices, and as well, serves on the Program Committee for the Canadian Moodlemoot. This is all part of her passion for this open source virtual learning environment. She has presented provincially, nationally, and internationally on topics related to teaching mathematics, online education, Moodle, and assessment.

Aside from working, Joan is part of a landscaping tree farm in Northwestern Alberta with her two children. She enjoys painting, making stained glass, travelling, skiing, and gardening in her free time.

About the Reviewers

Rafael Reyna Camones is a consultant of information technology. He has experience in the development of modules for Moodle and currently focuses on the integration of e-learning platform with mobile devices (iOS, Android, and Windows Phone).

He graduated as Systems Engineer from the Universidad Nacional José Faustino Sánchez Carrión. He has trained university staff in the use of Moodle and developed a pilot for implementation.

In his spare time he enjoys a good conversation and exchange of ideas.

David Le Blanc, BA, B.Ed, M.Ed, PhD (ABD)

David Le Blanc is an experienced online guide, Moodle expert, and e-learning practitioner. He has been working in computer-based learning since the mid '80s and in secondary education for the past 22 years. Currently, David works with local school districts and colleges to design online learning and to support educators to deliver courses in the Moodle learning environment.

www.PacktPub.com

Support files, eBooks, discount offers and more

You might want to visit www.PacktPub.com for support files and downloads related to your book.

Did you know that Packt offers eBook versions of every book published, with PDF and ePub files available? You can upgrade to the eBook version at www.PacktPub.com and as a print book customer, you are entitled to a discount on the eBook copy. Get in touch with us at service@packtpub.com for more details.

At www.PacktPub.com, you can also read a collection of free technical articles, sign up for a range of free newsletters and receive exclusive discounts and offers on Packt books and eBooks.

http://PacktLib.PacktPub.com

Do you need instant solutions to your IT questions? PacktLib is Packt's online digital book library. Here, you can access, read and search across Packt's entire library of books.

Why Subscribe?

- ▸ Fully searchable across every book published by Packt
- ▸ Copy and paste, print and bookmark content
- ▸ On demand and accessible via web browser

Free Access for Packt account holders

If you have an account with Packt at www.PacktPub.com, you can use this to access PacktLib today and view nine entirely free books. Simply use your login credentials for immediate access.

Table of Contents

Preface

Moodle is the leading open source learning management system. Moodle Quiz provides learners with effective ways to interact with course content. It is one of the core modules in Moodle and an impressive tool in achieving the goal of creating interactive, flexible online learning experiences that help learners take control of their educational environment.

Instant Moodle Quiz Module How-to shows you a variety of ways to use the Moodle Quiz tool to enhance your teaching and create meaningful educational experiences for your learners. When we think about creating quizzes, we are often focused on the test that demonstrates learning—assessment *of* learning (summative assessment). The quiz tool can do that, but so much more! As learners proceed through the course, they often want the answer to the question "how am I doing?" With careful design, instructors can use the Moodle Quiz tool to provide assessment *for* learning (formative assessment), providing feedback to the learners when they need it, independent of the instructor.

For more information on assessment, please visit `http://www.crcs.bc.ca/ teacherlinks/for-as-of.html`.

Moodle Quiz includes a full web page editor that can incorporate text, image, audio, and video files, allowing creativity and flexibility in creating questions.

Many instructors experience frustration on the first attempt to use the Moodle Quiz. After completing the configuration tasks, they discover that there is no content in the quiz. The reason for this is that the quiz tool depends on a well-organized question bank. We will begin this book by first setting up the question bank, and then creating a variety of quizzes from it. Generally, question bank development is best completed along with course development.

We choose questions from our question bank to create a Moodle quiz. The questions we put into the bank remain in place even when we delete a quiz.

Now let's talk about some options we have for using the Moodle Quiz tool:

- ▶ Create a quiz to evaluate learners' mastery of a unit or module of material.

- ▶ Use a quiz as a self check, with multiple attempts, for small segments of instructions. Allow the learners to access the self check at any time in the instruction. They may choose to use it as a pre-test, progress indicator, or mastery indicator.

- ▶ Use quiz in the Adaptive mode that allows the learners to attempt the question until they get it right. This is a good strategy for critical concepts required as a basis for further learning.

This book is a complete guide to using the powerful Moodle Quiz module for successful teaching and using the best educational practices for assessment encompassing assessment *for*, *as*, and *of* learning.

What this book covers

Creating categories in the question bank (Must know), explains how we can organize questions into categories for easy identification, retrieval, and re-use in the creation of quizzes. When we start using the Moodle Quiz tool, we will find it is optimized by creating a large pool of questions in the question bank.

Moving questions from one catogory to another (Must know), discusses how to move questions from one category to another.

Creating questions in the question bank (Must know), discusses a variety of question formats for creating questions to build the question bank. The question bank is really a database. The strength of the question bank is derived from how well it is organized, using categories and standard naming practices.

Types of questions (Must know), provides a variety of ways of asking questions and a rich selection of question types, which are required for an effective assessment, provided in the Moodle Quiz module. This is another great opportunity for collaborating with other instructors—creating a question bank together is a great way of seeing different points of view on assessment.

Adding feedback to questions (Should know), discusses about a valuable way to communicate with learners at a distance—feedback. Quiz allows us to provide feedback for the learner at multiple levels in the questions.

Configuring quiz settings 1 (Must know), examines the quiz settings 1 to 5 (out of nine different settings), explaining the significance of each choice. Moodle Quiz is a powerful tool that allows for many different design options.

Configuring quiz settings 2 (Must know), continues with our work on configuring the quiz as we examine settings 6 to 9 in this recipe, explaining the significance of each choice.

Creating the quiz (Must know), explains how to edit the quiz in tabbed page and select questions from the exam bank.

Displaying the quiz (Should know), the decisions made by the instructor, especially under the **Order and paging** tab, have an effect on how the finished quiz will be displayed.

Quiz from the learner's perspective (Must know), provides a chance to take a look at the quiz as the learner sees it. This includes the number of attempts, timelines, navigation, scoring, feedback, and flagged questions

Reviewing the quiz from the learner's perspective (Should know), discusses how to review the graded quiz from the learner's perspective. When a learner completes the quiz, it is graded. Here, we can see how our efforts and feedback decisions enhance learning opportunities within our quiz.

Quiz from the instructor's perspective (Should know), explains what the instructor sees once the learner has done the quiz. This allows the instructor to evaluate assessment choices (*for* and *of* learning), monitor learner progress, re-grade, and review class results.

Quiz security (Should know), discusses the quiz security issues, which include the Moodle Quiz settings and course design strategies.

Quiz reports (Become an expert), explains how to examine the **Grades**, **Responses**, **Statistics**, and **Manual grading** reports. Review and analysis of students' results is an important tool in improving instructions.

What you need for this book

We need a Moodle 2.x to use all features of the quiz that will be discussed. This book is intended for anyone who is designing instructions for learners. To make best use of this book a *Role of Teacher* in Moodle is needed—that means you have full ability to edit the Moodle courses.

Who this book is for

If you are creating any kind of instructions using Moodle as your Learning Management System, this book is for you! Step-by-step application of the features of Moodle Quiz provides a good grounding in creating effective assessment *for* and *of* learning. Strong assessment is one of the keys to effective instruction and successful learners. Readers are expected to have a basic working knowledge of Moodle and access to a course they can edit.

Conventions

In this book, you will find a number of styles of text that distinguish between different kinds of information. Here are some examples of these styles, and an explanation of their meaning.

Code words in text are shown as follows: "For example, if we enter `169.254.219.173`, the learner can access the quiz only from that single computer."

New terms and **important words** are shown in bold. Words that you see on the screen, in menus or dialog boxes for example, appear in the text like this: "Scroll to the bottom to the **Add category** area."

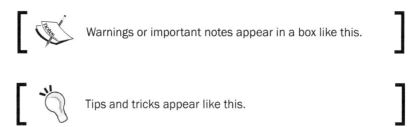

Warnings or important notes appear in a box like this.

Tips and tricks appear like this.

Reader feedback

Feedback from our readers is always welcome. Let us know what you think about this book—what you liked or may have disliked. Reader feedback is important for us to develop titles that you really get the most out of.

To send us general feedback, simply send an e-mail to `feedback@packtpub.com`, and mention the book title via the subject of your message.

If there is a book that you need and would like to see us publish, please send us a note in the **SUGGEST A TITLE** form on `www.packtpub.com` or e-mail `suggest@packtpub.com`.

If there is a topic that you have expertise in and you are interested in either writing or contributing to a book, see our author guide on `www.packtpub.com/authors`.

Customer support

Now that you are the proud owner of a Packt book, we have a number of things to help you to get the most from your purchase.

Errata

Although we have taken every care to ensure the accuracy of our content, mistakes do happen. If you find a mistake in one of our books—maybe a mistake in the text or the code—we would be grateful if you would report this to us. By doing so, you can save other readers from frustration and help us improve subsequent versions of this book. If you find any errata, please report them by visiting http://www.packtpub.com/support, selecting your book, clicking on the **errata submission form** link, and entering the details of your errata. Once your errata are verified, your submission will be accepted and the errata will be uploaded on our website, or added to any list of existing errata, under the Errata section of that title. Any existing errata can be viewed by selecting your title from http://www.packtpub.com/support.

Piracy

Piracy of copyright material on the Internet is an ongoing problem across all media. At Packt, we take the protection of our copyright and licenses very seriously. If you come across any illegal copies of our works, in any form, on the Internet, please provide us with the location address or website name immediately so that we can pursue a remedy.

Please contact us at copyright@packtpub.com with a link to the suspected pirated material.

We appreciate your help in protecting our authors, and our ability to bring you valuable content.

Questions

You can contact us at questions@packtpub.com if you are having a problem with any aspect of the book, and we will do our best to address it.

Instant Moodle Quiz Module How-to

Welcome to *Instant Moodle Quiz Module How-to*—a versatile tool.

This book will teach the readers how to make a quiz from scratch in Moodle, using the core Quiz module. It will examine applications of the Quiz tool, educational design for different purposes, and feedback for both learners and instructors. A variety of report formats provide opportunities for instructors to analyze the quiz results to improve the learning environment.

Creating categories in the question bank (Must know)

When we start using the Quiz tool, we will find that it is optimized by creating a large pool of questions in the question bank. We can organize questions into categories for easy identification, retrieval, and re-use in the creation of quizzes.

Getting ready

The **question bank** contains all the questions for the whole course. It is important to organize them into categories so that we can find the questions we want. This is also important when we want to use the random question feature in a quiz (to be discussed later). Many instructors create logical categories based on the desired outcomes of the course to provide useful groupings of questions.

The same question may be added to more than one category—however, since you may use multiple categories in creating the quiz, this practice seems a bit wasteful.

How to do it...

To create a question category, follow these steps:

1. Select **Settings** | **Course administration** | **Question bank** | **Categories**.

2. Scroll to the bottom to the **Add category** area.

3. Choose a category from the **Parent category** drop-down box:

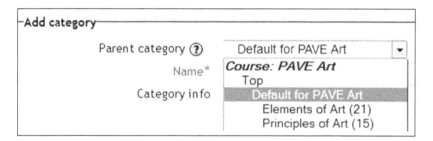

4. Notice that the **Top** category is **PAVE Art**—the name of the course. Already there are two categories under **PAVE Art**—lets add another.

5. In the **Name** field, enter a name for the new category and a description of the type of questions in the category:

Add category

Parent category ⑦	Default for PAVE Art ▾
Name*	Elements of Art - Applications
Category info	Questions about the applications of the elements of art in artworks.

Add category

6. Click on the **Add category** button and our new category will be added.

Question categories for 'Course: PAVE Art '

- Default for PAVE Art (0) The default category for questions shared in context 'PAVE Art . ✗ ✎
  - Elements of Art (21) Questions dealing with definitions of Elements of Art. ✗ ✎ ← ↓
  - Elements of Art - Applications (0) Questions about the applications of the elements of art in artworks. ✗ ✎ ← ↑ ↓ →
  - Principles of Art (15) Questions dealing with definitions of Principles of Art. ✗ ✎ ← ↑ →

The number in brackets following each category name indicates the number of questions in that category. Notice that there are zero questions in the category we just created.

At any time we can edit the categories by clicking on the ✎ icon.

How it works...

It is important to take a look at the outcomes in the course we are teaching and create categories as outlined in the *How to do it...* section, which groups our essential ideas in a logical fashion. There are always questions about the appropriate size of categories—our guideline is manageable chunks of learning.

There's more...

Sometimes, as we refine our categories, we will discover that a question would be better in a different category.

Moving questions from one category to another (Must know)

It is easy to move questions between categories.

When reviewing questions in the categories created for the **PAVE Art** course, we decided the second question in **Elements of Art Definitions** was really an application question and belonged in another category. How do we move a question from one category to another?

How to do it...

Follow these steps to move questions from one category to another:

1. Select **Settings | Course administration | Question bank | Questions**:

2. Let's take a look at the question we want to move. This is a question dealing with texture in art and is more an application than a definition. Choose the category at the top of the page:

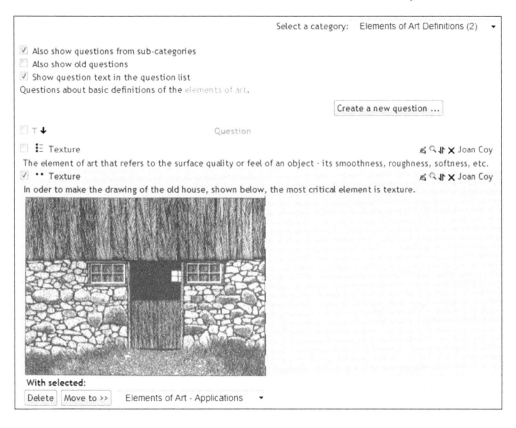

3. To move a question to another category, click on the box beside the question to select it.

4. At the bottom, select the new category for the question.

5. Click on the **Move to** button.

How it works...

We now have our question in the appropriate category. The organization by categories is very important for effective use of Moodle Quiz as all questions used are drawn from the question bank. We may find it useful to create a standard practice for naming questions for easy identification and retrieval—especially, if we are sharing courses with fellow instructors.

If you want to learn more, go to `http://docs.moodle.org/21/en/Question_categories`.

Creating questions in the question bank (Must know)

Now we are ready to start adding questions to the question bank. Moodle Quiz provides a variety of question formats for creating questions to build the question bank. The question bank is really a database. The strength of the question bank is derived from how well it is organized, using categories and standard naming practices.

Getting ready

We want to begin by organizing the questions that we create into appropriate categories in the question bank. The ability to categorize questions within the question bank will greatly enhance the use of the tool to easily generate different quizzes. Of course, this task is easier if we already have some questions or at least a good idea of the kind of questions that we want to add to the question bank.

How to do it...

Follow these steps for creating a question:

1. Select **Settings** | **Course administration** | **Question bank** | **Questions**:

2. Select the category for your question from the top of the page:

3. Click on **Create a new question...** and select the type of question you want from the pop-up window.

4. When we select a question type, a brief description will appear—we are creating a multiple choice question.

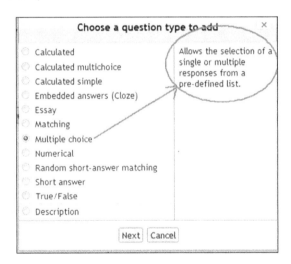

5. Click on the **Next** button, which will bring you to the web editing page where we can add the question information and possible responses.

Let's add a new multiple choice question to our question bank:

1. The question name is seen only by the instructor. It is a good idea to make it clear and descriptive, so you can easily locate questions when you are creating a quiz.

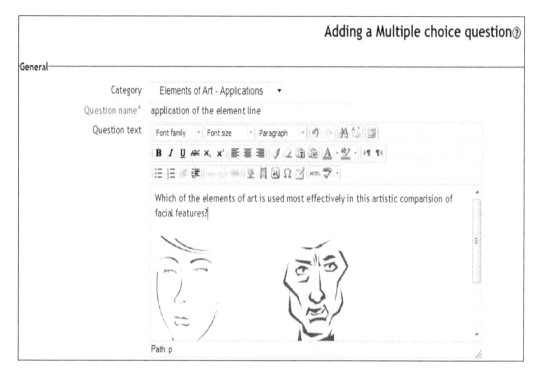

2. The **question text** is the actual question that the learner will see.
3. The choices are the possible answers to the question. We may choose to have one answer (worth **100%**) or more than one answer. If, for example, we have two correct answers, each answer would be worth **50%**.

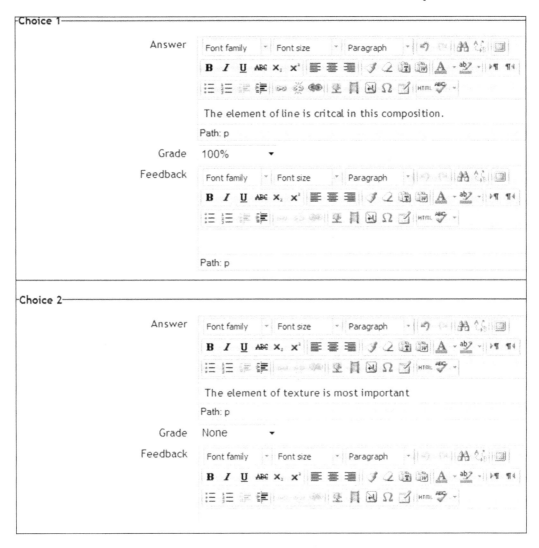

We are creating a question that has just one correct answer and it will be graded at **100%**. Choice 1 is the correct answer and we have weighted it at **100%**. If we had created a question with two correct answers, each correct answer would be weighted at **50%**, adding up to a total of **100%**.

The **One or multiple answers?** drop down shows the default of **One answer only**:

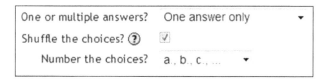

We have also chosen to shuffle the choices—that means when we create the quiz, we can have the order of the choices changed every time the quiz is displayed. Finally, we have chosen to have the choices for the multiple choice questions labeled with lower case letters.

4. When we have completed our question creation, click on **Save Changes** at the very bottom. This question will then be added to the category in the question bank that we chose at the beginning.

How it works...

We have worked with the question bank to learn how it forms the basis for the Moodle Quiz and the site from which all quiz questions are drawn. We have chosen to create a multiple choice question among the many question formats that can populate our question bank. A rich question bank is essential to effectively use the powerful Moodle Quiz tool.

There's more...

The effectiveness and flexibility of using the Moodle Quiz tool increases along with the development of a rich question bank. As we become more familiar with adding questions to the question bank, we find it easier to accommodate the different ways in which learners can learn. This is an excellent opportunity for instructors of similar subject areas to collaborate in the development and share their questions.

Sharing your questions across different sites

We can share questions across different sites by using the Export and Import functions. We can export questions to a file saved on our computer and then import these into a different course site. They will appear in the question bank of the new site, and can then be moved and edited accordingly.

For more information, go to `http://docs.moodle.org/23/en/Question_types`.

Types of questions (Must know)

We have a multitude of different question types that we can use for creating a quiz. It is important to understand our options and strategies for using them.

Effective assessment requires a variety of ways of asking questions and there is a rich selection of question types provided in the Moodle Quiz module. This is another great opportunity for collaboration with other instructors—creating a question bank together is a great way of seeing different points of view on assessment.

Getting ready

There are many question types—some are more advanced than others.

Matching	The answer to each subquestion must be selected from a list of possibilities.	The instructor creates a list of subquestions and the answer to each subquestion. The learner must match each correct answer to the question.
Embedded answers (Cloze)	Questions of this type are very flexible, and are created by entering text containing special codes that create multiple choice, short answers and numerical questions. The student is presented with text where some words are missing (cloze text). The student fills in the missing text by typing it in or by selecting it from a drop down.	This is an advanced format. More information can be found at `http://docs.moodle.org/21/en/Embedded_Answers_%28Cloze%29_question_type#Format`.
Essay	Allows a response of a few sentences or paragraphs. This must then be graded manually.	For the essay question, the learner can have the Moodle rich text editor as long as the instructor ensures only one essay question per page. That means the rich text editor will be turned off if the instructor prefers to display multiple essay questions per page This is graded manually.

For more information on quiz question types, go to `http://docs.moodle.org/23/en/Question_types`.

How to do it...

Let's take a look at the steps for creating a few types of questions.

1. For a matching question, the question text is entered into the editor, just like the multiple choice question that we created earlier. The choices are created differently. These questions deal with descriptive statements of various elements of art.

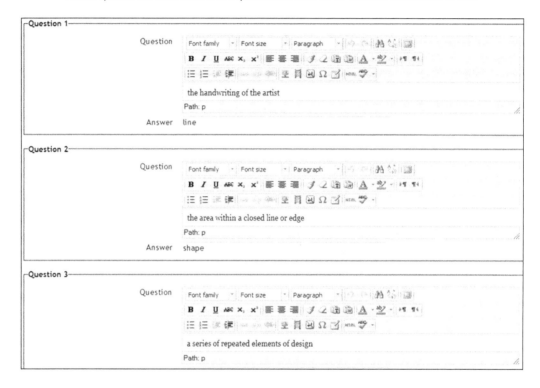

2. For the matching format, the questions are displayed with the answers in a drop-down box from which the learners can select their choice.

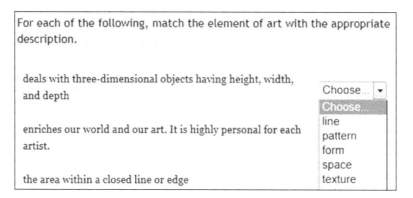

3. If we want to have more choices than questions, we can enter answers with blank questions.

4. Using the embedded answers (Cloze) question type, we can create multiple choice questions that display a drop down similar to the matching question we just created. This is an advanced question format and requires text entered in the Moodle format containing various answers embedded in it. Note the special format required, as shown in the following example:

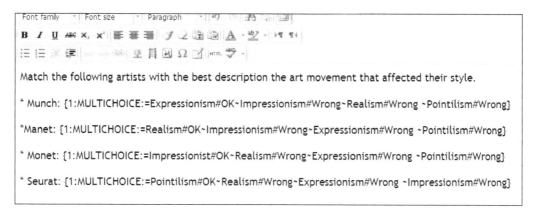

5. The learner is given the opportunity to choose the best answer from a drop down in each case.

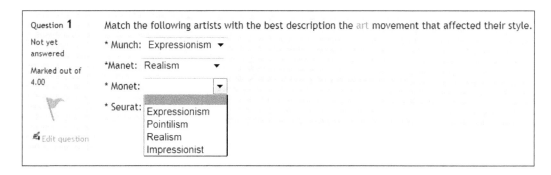

6. For more information on the embedded answers (Cloze) question type, go to `http://docs.moodle.org/21/en/Embedded_Answers_%28Cloze%29_question_type#Format`.

7. For an essay question, an instructor enters the question text by using the web page editor. This question requires the learner to respond in a paragraph or a few sentences. We need to make some decisions about designing the response area for the learner.

An interesting feature of the essay question in Moodle is that, for the student to have the HTML editor, the instructor must ensure that each essay question is on a separate page in the quiz presentation.

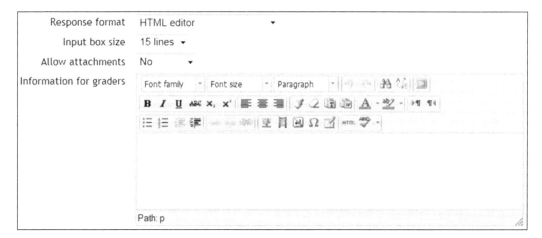

▶ In **Response format**, we can choose between HTML editor and text only. The HTML editor will allow image, audio, and video files as well as text in the learner response.

▶ **Input box size** allows us to set a limit on the response between 5 and 40 lines.

▸ The **Allow attachments** drop down allows us to determine whether or not attachments are allowed and the ability to specify how many are allowed.

When we understand the wide variety of question types provided in the Moodle Quiz module, we are better equipped to create effective, formative, and summative assessments for our learners. The range of question types facilitates assessing topics from basic knowledge and skills to critical thinking and problem solving.

There's more...

When we are creating questions, we can also add tags to make it easier to search our exam banks for questions.

Tags	Official tags (Manage official tags)
	Art
	Other tags (enter tags separated by commas)
	Elements, Applications

Official tags appear site wide and require the administrator role to add them. Other tags may be added by the teacher, but these are restricted to the current question bank.

Adding feedback to questions (Should know)

Feedback is a valuable way to communicate with learners at a distance. Quiz allows us to provide feedback for the learner at multiple levels in the questions.

Getting ready

Any learner taking a quiz may want to know how well he/she has answered the questions posed. Often, working with Moodle, the instructor is at a distance from the learner. Providing feedback is a great way of enhancing communication between learner and instructor.

Learner feedback can be provided at multiple levels using Moodle Quiz. You can create feedback at various levels in both the questions and the overall quiz. Here we will examine feedback at the question level.

General feedback

When we add General Feedback to a question, every student sees the feedback, regardless of their answer to the question. This is good opportunity to provide clarification for the learner who had guessed a correct answer, as well as for the learner whose response was incorrect.

Individual response feedback

We can create feedback tailored to each possible response in a multiple choice question. This feedback can be more focused in nature. Often, a carefully crafted distracter in a multiple choice can reveal misconceptions and the feedback can provide the correction required as soon as the learner completes the quiz. Feedback given when the question is fresh in the learner's mind, is very effective.

How to do it...

Let's create some learner feedback for some of the questions that we have created in the question bank:

1. First of all, let's add general feedback to a question.

2. Returning to our *True-False question* on *Texture*, we can see that general feedback is effective when there are only two choices.

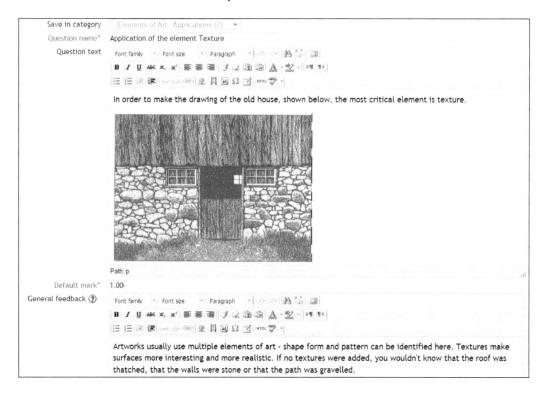

3. Remember that this type of feedback will appear for all learners, regardless of the answer they submitted. The intention of this feedback is to reflect the correct solution and also give more background information to enhance the teaching opportunity.

4. Let's take a look at how to create a specific feedback for each possible response that a learner may submit. This is done by adding individual response feedback.

5. Returning to our multiple choice question on **application of the element line**, a specific feedback response tailored to each possible choice will provide helpful clarification for the student. This type of feedback is entered after each possible choice.

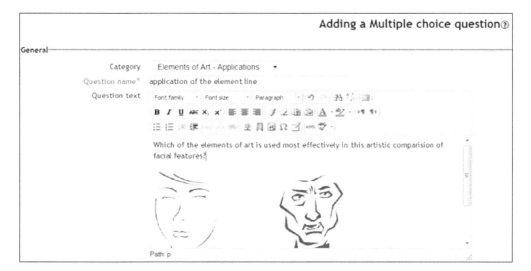

6.   Here is an example of a feedback to reinforce a correct response and a feedback for an incorrect response:

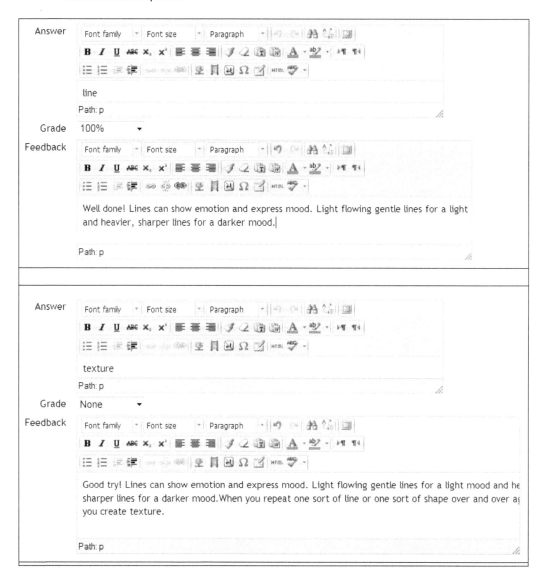

7.   In this case, the feedback the learner receives is tailored to the response they have submitted. This provides much more specific feedback to the learner's choice of responses.

8.   For the embedded question (Cloze), feedback is easy to add in Moodle 2.0. In the following screenshot, we can see the question that we created with feedback added:

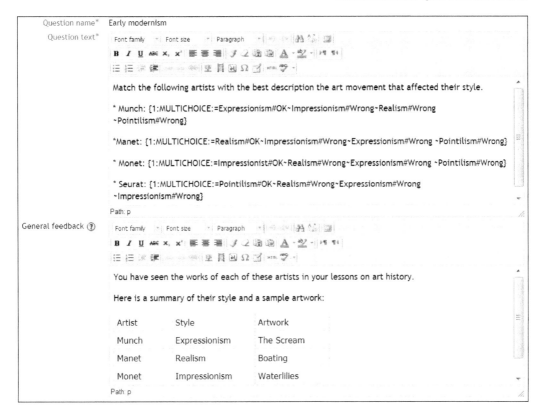

9. And this is what the feedback looks like to the student:

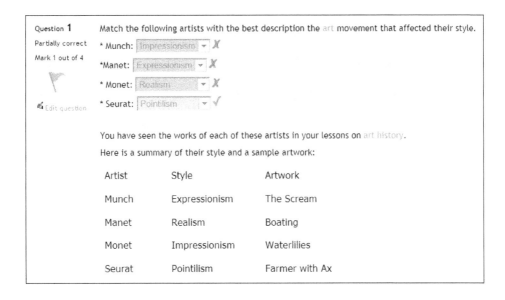

How it works...

We have now improved questions in our exam bank by providing feedback for the learner. We have created both general feedback that all learners will see and specific feedback for each response the learner may choose. As we think about the learning experience for the learner, we can see that immediate feedback with our questions is an effective way to reinforce learning. This is another feature that makes Moodle Quiz such a powerful tool.

There's more...

As we think about the type of feedback we want for the learner, we can combine feedback for individual responses with general feedback. Also there are options for feedback for any correct response, for any partially correct response, or for any incorrect response. Feedback serves to engage the learners and personalize the experience.

We created question categories, organized our questions into categories, and learned how to add learner feedback at various levels inside the questions. We are now ready to configure a quiz.

Configuring quiz settings 1 (Must know)

Moodle Quiz is a powerful tool that allows for many different design options. We will examine quiz settings 1 to 5, explaining the significance of each choice.

Getting ready

The first step in creating a quiz is its configuration. The decisions we make here play an important role in determining the purpose for the quiz and how the learners will experience it.

There are nine quiz settings to consider. We will begin with the first five.

In the **General** section, we first give the quiz a name and description. We then decide if the quiz is always open or will be available only on specific dates. We can set a time limit, if desired, determine the number of attempts allowed, and choose the grading method.

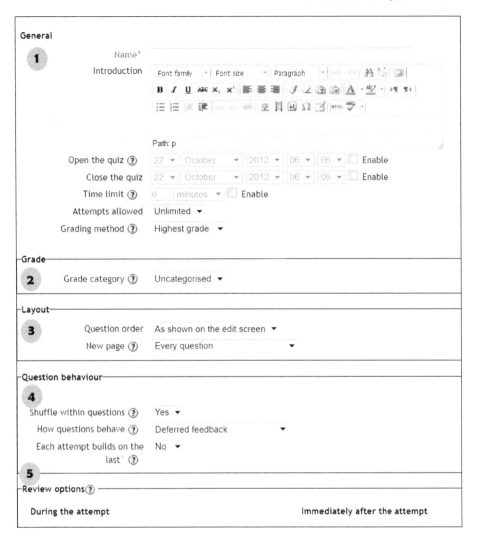

Grade allows us to assign a value to the quiz that will be represented in the Moodle Grade book.

Layout allows us to determine the order in which the questions will appear and where page breaks will occur in the quiz.

> ▸ **Question order**: We can choose to have the quiz questions appear in just the same order that we chose on the edit screen. Alternatively, we can choose to have them displayed randomly so that the order of questions changes each time the quiz is displayed.

> ▸ **New page**: Here we can determine the number of questions that are displayed on each page for the learner. This allows us to group the questions for the best presentation of our quiz. Page breaks will be inserted according to this setting; however, we can also control the page breaks from the editing screen when adding questions. We may choose to have no page breaks, so that all questions are presented on a single screen. Note that the default is one question per page. Remember that this is the best choice when presenting multiple essay type questions on a single page to ensure that learners will have access to the rich text editor for each essay question.

Our decisions in the **Question behaviour** section will influence how the learner experiences the quiz. We may choose to shuffle the possible responses to discourage students from collaborating when taking the same quiz.

There are four main behaviors:

> ▸ **Deferred feedback**: The learner enters answers for all questions, submits the entire quiz before grading, and then he/she gets the access to feedback.

> ▸ **Immediate feedback**: The learner submits each question as they go and receives grading and feedback right away.

> ▸ **Interactive feedback with multiple tries**: The learner submits each question as they go and receives immediate feedback. The learner can then submit another try, perhaps for a reduced grade.

> ▸ **Adaptive mode**: The learner is given multiple chances for each question. We can create a message to display when the learner answers incorrectly and then display a new question on the same content. Alternatively, we can simply redisplay the same question when the learner answers incorrectly.

In **Review options**, the instructor can control the nature of the feedback the learner receives after the quiz is complete and when it occurs.

Time of review	What it means
During the attempt	Feedback is only available when **How questions behave** has been set to **Immediate feedback**, **Immediate feedback with CBM**, and/or **Interactive feedback with multiple tries**. If set to one of these options, then a **Check** button will appear below the answer that the students can check to submit their response and receive immediate feedback.
Immediately after the attempt	Means within 2 minutes of the student clicking on **Submit all and finish**.
Later, while the quiz is still open	Means after 2 minutes of submitting and finishing the quiz attempt, but before the close date. If the quiz does not have a close date, this phase will never end.
After the quiz is closed	Means what it says (you never get here for quizzes without a close date).

 Note: Quote from `http://docs.moodle.org/22/en/Quiz_ settings#Review_options`.

How to do it...

Let's take a look at setting up a quiz in our Art course.

To add a quiz, turn on editing, go to **Add an activity...**, and click on **Quiz**:

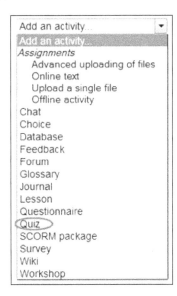

This will open the **Adding a new Quiz** settings page. This page is divided into nine areas. Let's go through the first five in this section.

▸ **General**: These settings are shown in the following screenshot:

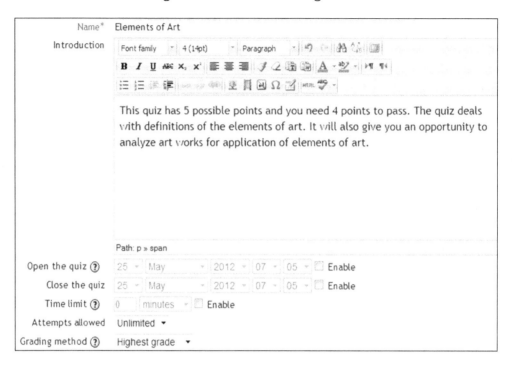

- ❑ **Name**: This is the title of the quiz **Elements of Art** and is displayed on the course's home page.

- ❑ **Introduction**: Here we communicate with the learner about the quiz as well as any important features they need to know before beginning. It will appear for the learner when they click on the quiz title before attempting the quiz.

- ❑ **Open the Quiz/Close the Quiz**: These dates determine when the quiz is open to the learners. We did not choose open and close dates and so the quiz is always open.

- ❑ **Time limit**: A time limit can be set for a quiz. When the limit is reached, the quiz is automatically submitted with the responses completed at that time. By default, the quiz does not have a time limit, A time limit can be set for a quiz. When the limit is reached, the quiz is automatically submitted with the completed responses at that time. We will choose the default of no time limit.

- ❑ **Attempts allowed**; The number of times a learner can take a quiz can be set here. We are allowing an **Unlimited** number of attempts as this quiz is intended for assessment *for* learning.

- ❑ **Grading method**: There are four options for how the quiz is graded. We have chosen **Highest grade** as our goal is mastery learning.

▸ **Grade**: This setting provides the connection for this quiz to the Moodle Gradebook. For example, in this case, we have a common High School Art course with different assessments for each grade level. In this case, we would choose **Art 10** and then this quiz would appear for learners taking Art 10, but not for learners in Art 20 and Art 30. Don't worry if categories in Gradebook are not yet set up—there is an opportunity to do that when we work with Gradebook. If that is the case, we just leave the quiz as **Uncategorised**.

▸ **Layout**: This area controls how the questions appear on the screen for the learner.

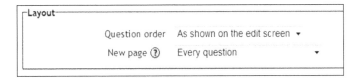

We have chosen to display the questions just as they appear on the edit page with a new page for every question.

▸ **Question behaviour**:

- ❑ **Shuffle within question**: When we enable this setting, it means that parts of a question such as multiple choice will be randomly shuffled each time the quiz is displayed. There are, however, two conditions.

In the question itself, the **Shuffle the choices?** checkbox must be checked.

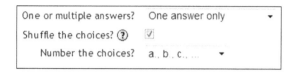

There must be something to shuffle so that multiple choice and matching would work, but it would have no effect on numericals, short answers, or essay questions.

❑ **How questions behave**: We have quite a bit of control over how the quiz questions behave and hence over the experience for the learner. We have chosen to give learners feedback after the quiz is complete.

❑ **Each attempt builds on the last**: If multiple attempts are allowed and this setting is enabled, each new quiz attempt will contain the results of the previous attempt. This allows a quiz to be completed over several attempts. We have decided not to use this feature for this quiz.

▸ **Review options**: We have a number of choices here. It is generally a good idea to begin with the default settings and refine our choices as we build experience with the quiz behavior and our learners.

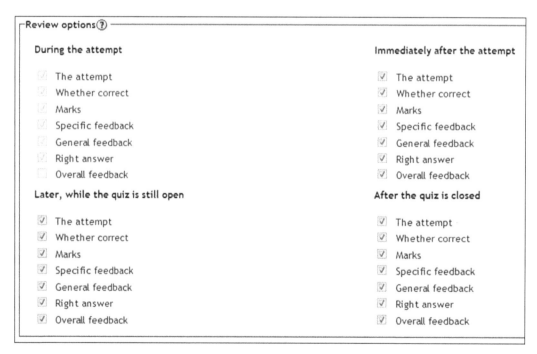

The following table explains the effect of each of the choices:

Choice	Explanation
The attempt	Will show how the student responded to each question.
Whether correct	Displays whether the student's response to each question is correct or incorrect.
Marks	Reveals the marks awarded to the student and the grade for the quiz.
Specific feedback	Will show the feedback for the response to the question as set when adding the question to the quiz. Each response to a question can have feedback for both correct and incorrect answers.
General feedback	Displays the general feedback for the whole question as set when adding the question to the quiz. You can use the general feedback to give students some background to what knowledge the question was testing.
Right answer	Reveals the correct answer to each question, whether the student answered correctly or not.
Overall feedback	Displays feedback for the entire quiz as set in the quiz settings.

 Note: Quote from `http://docs.moodle.org/22/en/Quiz_ settings#Review_options`.

How it works...

We have made some important decisions in the configuration of our quiz including what the learner sees on opening the quiz, when the quiz is open, time limits, number of attempts, grading, layout of quiz, nature of feedback, and possibilities for review. These are some important decisions for us to make, all of which have an impact on the learner's experience of the quiz. Happily, we can alter these decisions even after we have created the quiz.

Configuring quiz settings 2 (Must know)

We will continue with our work on configuring the quiz as we examine settings 6 to 9, explaining the significance of each choice.

Getting ready

We are ready to work through the last four sections on the quiz configuration.

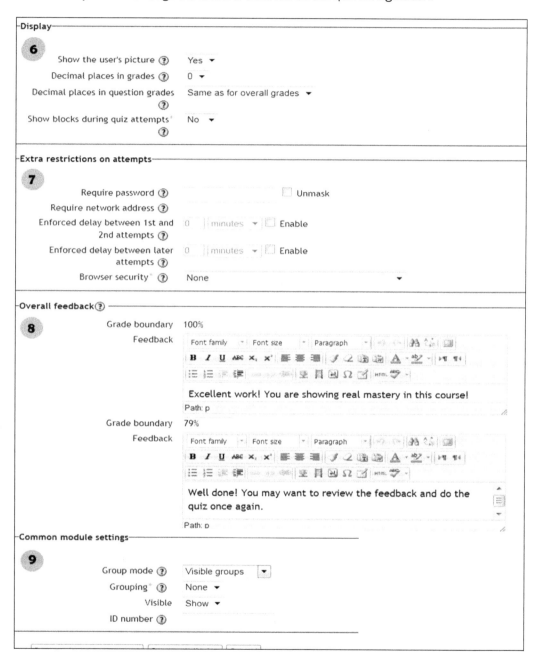

In the **Display** section, we can decide whether or not to show the learner's profile picture during the quiz attempt and quiz review.

By default, blocks displayed on the course page will be hidden during the quiz attempts unless switched to **Yes** in this section.

Let's take a look at some of the decisions that we can make in the **Display** section:

- **Show the user's picture**: If **Yes** is chosen here, the learner's name and profile picture will be displayed while the learner is taking the quiz.

- **Decimal places in grades**: This setting determines the number of decimal places in the grades for the students. The first setting is for the overall grade, while the second is the grade for each question. These settings affect only the display, Moodle quiz still calculates grades with full accuracy.

- **Show blocks during quiz attempts**: This setting allows the instructor to determine whether or not the course blocks will be displayed during the quiz.

The instructor can choose added security features, using **Extra restrictions on attempts** to require a password, restrict to specific IP addresses, or implement a secure browser during quiz administration. We can make a number of choices, in the **Extra restrictions on attempts** section, to tailor the quiz experience for the learner.

- **Require password**: We may require the learner to enter a password in order to be able to take the quiz. If **Unmask** is checked, the password will be shown—handy for the instructor, in case a password is forgotten.

- **Require network address**: The instructor can require the learner to access the quiz from a particular IP address. For example, if we enter 169.254.219.173, the learner can do the quiz only from that single computer. If this is our school, then entering 169.254 would allow a range of IP addresses in our school, but nowhere else.

- **Enforced delay between 1st and 2nd attempts** and **Enforced delay between later attempts**: These two settings allow the instructor to determine a delay time between multiple quiz attempts. Of course, this applies only when the instructor has enabled multiple attempts for the quiz.

- **Browser security**: If the setting, **Full screen pop-up with some Java-Script security** is used, the quiz is launched in a new window. Java-Script is used to disable copying, saving, and printing of the quiz.

Overall feedback allows us to give the student a message dictated by grade boundaries after the quiz is complete.

In **Common module settings**, we can use some of the course settings such as **Grouping** and **ID number**.

> ▸ **Group mode**: There are three different ways in which courses can be set up for grouping the students.
>
> > ❏ **No groups**: Everyone is grouped together in the course.
> >
> > ❏ **Separate groups**: Each member sees only the members in their group in the course.
> >
> > ❏ **Visible groups**: Each member works with their own group, but can see members of other groups.
>
> If a grouping of certain groups is created, students within these groupings can be assigned distinct activities and made visible only to members of the grouping.
>
> ▸ **ID number**: An ID number can be a way of identifying an activity for grading purposes. This can also be set in the Gradebook, if required.

How to do it...

We will continue with the decisions for the setup of our Art quiz.

> ▸ **Display**: In this section, we can choose options that affect information shown when the learner takes the quiz.

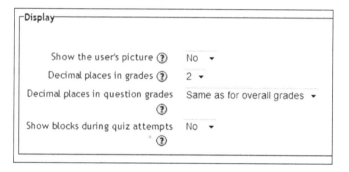

This section affects the way the student will see the quiz. Since we are creating a self check, security is not important and so we choose not to show the user's picture. We choose a consistent two decimal places for grades. Since we have art definitions in blocks in the course, we do not want to show blocks during the quiz attempt.

▶ **Extra restrictions on attempts**: This area is particularly useful when the security of quiz administration is a concern.

We have several levels of security available. First we decide whether or not to require a password. Since it is a self check, we decide not to use this. Then, we look at a higher level of security by requiring a network address—this limits the learner to a particular computer. We can enforce a time delay between multiple attempts at the quiz. In our case, we choose to leave that in the learner's control. We can also restrict the learner's ability to copy, save, and print the quiz by enabling **Browser security**.

▶ **Overall feedback**: We have already provided feedback at various levels within our quiz questions. Here we can offer general feedback, governed by grade boundaries. This is another level of feedback—this time at the level of the entire quiz grade. It is governed by grade boundaries.

For example, in the following illustration, if the learner achieves a score from **80%** to **100%**, the comment **Excellent work! You are showing real mastery of this course work!** will be displayed, whereas if the grade is from **65%** to **79%**, the comment will be **Well done! You may want to review the feedback and do the quiz once again**. This does not affect the comments created in each quiz question.

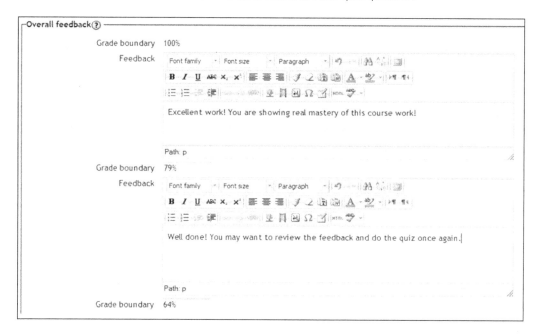

- ▶ **Common module settings**: This section allows us to use some settings made in the overall course.

  Here you can choose whether the quiz should be organized by group or not. This only has an effect on the review screens of the teachers where it determines which groups of students they see.

In our sample Art course, students from Art 10, Art 20, and Art 30 are in the same course, and groups are used to accommodate the various levels. We could reflect these groups in the quiz settings; however, as this is a self check for everyone, we will choose **No groups**.

How it works...

We have completed configuring our quiz. Our learner's experience with this quiz is affected by our decisions. The learner's photo and any blocks in the course will not appear. Learners will not require a password or other security and have no restrictions on when multiple quiz attempts may be made. Learners are provided with extensive, immediate feedback to support the learning process.

All the decisions made during the quiz configuration allow us to create quizzes that vary from a relaxed assessment *for* learning to a very controlled and secure assessment *of* learning. Remember, we can alter these decisions even after we have created the quiz, and that is a good thing as we learn from our experience with quizzes.

Creating the quiz (Must know)

After completing all of the settings to configure the quiz, it is time to edit the quiz's tabbed page and select questions from the exam bank.

Getting ready

We have spent considerable time in creating categories in our exam bank and populating those categories with appropriate questions. We then made many decisions in setting up the quiz.

There are a few things to notice on our quiz editing screen. One thing to keep in mind is that there is usually more than one way to do what we want when using Moodle.

- **Question bank contents**: When we click on **Show**, it takes us to the categories and questions that we have already created, so we can choose questions for this quiz

- **Maximum grade**: The overall grade for this quiz set by the instructor as well as weighting of each question

- **Add a question**: Another opportunity to add new questions to our Moodle course—this will be added directly to the quiz and will also be added to the question bank, and should be assigned to an appropriate category

- **Add a random question**: This allows addition of questions to the quiz, so that each time the quiz is started, questions are chosen at random from the category in the question bank specified by the instructor

How to do it...

Now it is time for us to create the quiz content by adding, weighting, and arranging questions.

Let's create a quiz together. It is important to keep in mind the purpose of the quiz—this one is intended to be a self check. We are hoping that learners will use it to master the terminology of the elements of art and begin to analyze the art works to see the use of the elements. With these goals in mind, we will make a short quiz with three attempts allowed and request a score of 80 percent to demonstrate mastery. We will set shuffled questions for the quiz.

1. Once we have configured the quiz, click on **Save and Display** and we will get a screen similar to the one shown in the following screenshot:

It shows the quiz name, introduction, attempts allowed, and grading method. It also tells the instructor that no questions have been added yet. It is now time to add questions to the quiz.

2. Click on **Edit quiz** to do this.

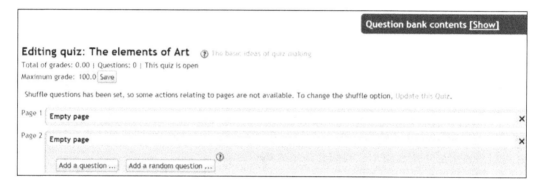

3. Let's take a look at the question bank contents:

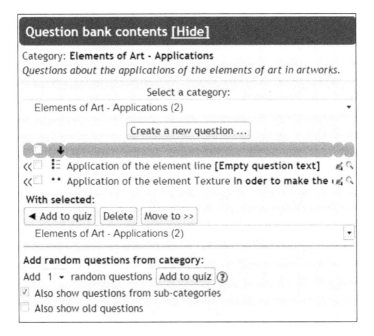

- We can see categories displayed at the top. The default is the whole course category, but we can choose the category we wish from the drop down.

  Once again we have the opportunity to create a new question. Notice that at any time we can edit existing questions by clicking on the ⬜ icon.

  To preview the question (see what the learner will see), click the ⚲ icon.

- By clicking in the little box available with each question, we can select specific questions to add to the quiz. Here, questions can also be deleted or moved to another category.

- We can also add random questions from a chosen category. Note that the random question has its own **Add to quiz** button.

- We can design a quiz that has some chosen questions and some random questions—or any combination we wish.

4. Let's go to the category of the **Elements of Art definitions** and choose a matching question to be on each quiz. Click on **Add to quiz**.

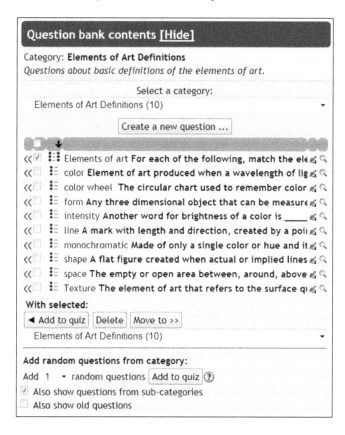

5. Then add three random questions from the same category and click on **Add to quiz**. Notice that there are 10 questions in this category and that will give us a reasonable selection. We can add random questions from different categories on the same quiz.

 We will get an error message, if we try to select a larger number of random questions than the category contains.

Notice that there are now four questions on the quiz—one selected and three that are random. That means we specified all questions on one page in the quiz configuration.

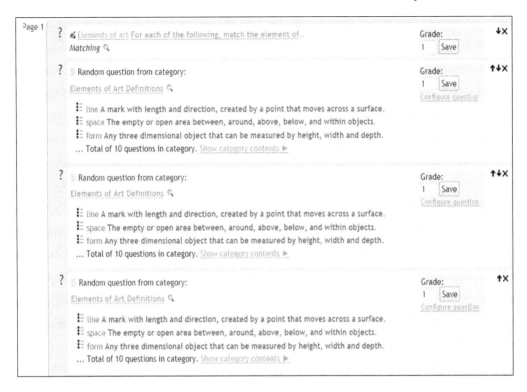

6. Now, we change the category to **Elements of Art - Applications** and we want to add one more random question. Remember to click on **Add to quiz** beside the random question.

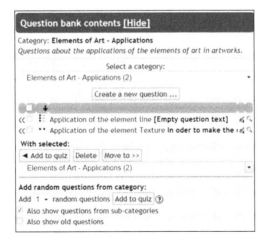

In this category, there are only two questions—not really enough to give students variety. The good news is that any additional questions we add to the category will be available for random question selection on new iterations of the quiz. Time to visit some fellow art teachers for question sharing!

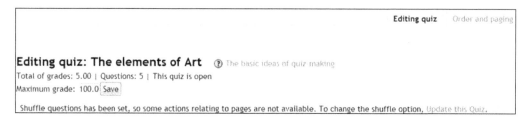

7. We need to set the weighting for each question. We can set the number of points for each question in the **Grade** area and we can make some questions worth more than others. It is important to save the grade at each question as we establish the weighting. Remember the questions will be weighted to match the total points possible that we set for the quiz. When we set the maximum grade to **100**, results are reported in percentage. When we review our quiz, we may decide that the grade per question needs to be changed. The matching question is multipart and the application question is more challenging. Here is the adjusted weighting:

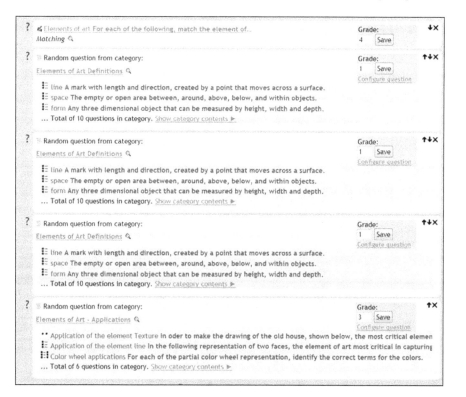

8. Click on **Save** and now the quiz is complete.

> **Editing quiz: The elements of Art** ⑦ The basic ideas of quiz-making
> Total of grades: 10.00 | Questions: 5 | This quiz is open
> Maximum grade: 100.0 Save
>
> Shuffle questions has been set, so some actions relating to pages are not available. To change the shuffle option, Update this Quiz.

Notice that the raw score for this quiz is 10 marks. For the gradebook purposes, this represents 100 percent and that is reflected in the maximum grade setting.

How it works...

We started with a quiz that was configured as we wished, but contained no questions. We added questions to our quiz from the question bank, guided by the categories organized for our questions. We arranged the questions as desired, created appropriate grading, and saved the completed quiz. We now have a quiz ready for our learners.

There's more...

When we are creating a quiz, we need to keep our purpose in mind. A quiz created as a self check may involve very different design decisions than one intended as a summative unit test.

Displaying the quiz (Should know)

The decisions made by the instructor, especially in the **Order and paging** tab, have an effect on how the finished quiz will be displayed.

Getting ready

We can control the way the learner will experience the quiz:

It is important to preview the quiz and spend a bit of time in fine-tuning how the quiz will be displayed.

How to do it...

Perform the following steps to decide the way in which the quiz will be displayed:

1. We will take a closer look at the order of questions and the pagination in this quiz. These are two features that will significantly affect the display of the quiz for our learners.

2. It is a good idea to preview the quiz before we decide it is complete. Go to our course and click on the quiz. We will be given the opportunity to attempt the quiz in preview mode.

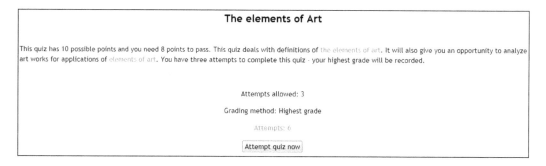

3. To further edit the quiz display, perform the following steps:
   1. Select **Settings** | **Quiz administration** | **Edit Quiz**.
   2. At the top of the page, select the **Order and paging** tab.
   3. Here we can examine the order of the questions and revisit decisions about pagination.

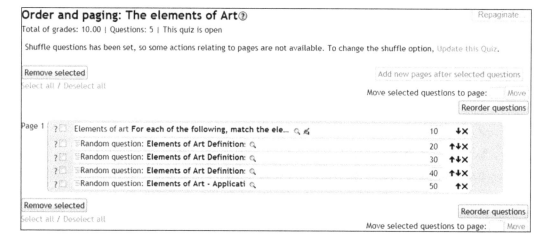

We can change the order of any question by using the upward/downward arrows, or alternately, by changing a value in one of the number order boxes. For instance, the teacher could move the *Application* question directly below the Matching question by replacing **50** with a value between 10 and 20 and clicking on the **Reorder questions** button. In the quiz that we are creating, we would like to have the *Matching* question first. The *Application* question should be last. For the random questions from *Elements of Art Definitions*, reordering does not have an effect.

4. Go to the update quiz. Then, in the **Layout** section, change the layout to correspond to the order we set in the edit screen, and click on **Save and display**.

┌─**Layout**───┐
│   │
│   Question order   As shown on the edit screen ▾   │
│   │
│   New page ⑦   Never, all questions on one page ▾ ☐ Repaginate now │
│   │
└──┘

┌─**Layout**───┐
│   │
│   Question order   Shuffled randomly   ▾   │
│   │
│   New page ⑦   Never, all questions on one page ▾ ☐ Repaginate now │
│   │
└──┘

5. When we look at the **Order and paging** tab in the edit screen, the questions now appear in the order we would like.

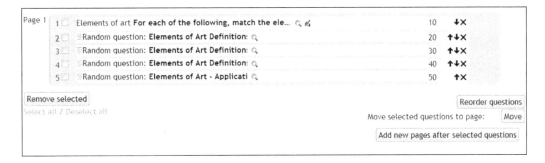

6. In this quiz, all of the questions are on one page, and this can work. However, if a learner's computer freezes during the quiz before they have submitted it, they will lose all answers selected on that page before that time. It would likely be a good idea to have the matching question on its own page. The application question will have a graphic and would also be good on one page.

7. To add a new page, perform the following steps:

    1. Select a question for which we want the new page to follow.

    2. Click on the **Add new pages after selected questions** button.

3. We will select questions 1 and 4 to add a new page after each one.

 If we select several questions, a new page will be added after each one.

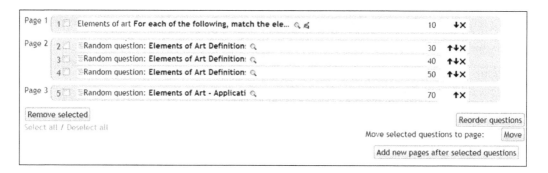

8. Now the questions are ordered as we want and pagination is correct. It is time to check the quiz by using a preview to see if it is displayed in the way we want for the learner.

How it works...

Upon reviewing our quiz, we are able to improve the display for the learner. First, we change the order of the questions so that they are organized in a logical way for learners. Then we change the quiz from having all questions on one page to presenting the quiz in several pages. This simplifies the appearance of the quiz and reduces the likelihood of learners losing work in the case of an interruption in computer service. Our choices at this point directly affect the way the quiz is displayed to the learners.

There's more...

The time we spend in reviewing the quiz before we open it to the learner is very important. Once our quiz has been attempted, we can no longer change questions or structure in the quiz. Happily, if we discover an error in a question, we can make the necessary changes in the question bank. Of course, we will likely have to re-grade for some learners—we'll learn about that in a future recipe.

Quiz from the learner's perspective (Must know)

This is a chance to take a look at the quiz as the learner sees it. This includes the number of attempts, timelines, navigation, scoring, feedback, and flagged questions.

Getting ready

Well, we have done it! Our quiz is ready and we can use a test student to see how the quiz works for the learner. It is interesting to see how all of our decisions play out in the learner context.

How to do it...

Of course, all the work we have been doing is only important in the hands of the learner.

How the learner will experience the quiz is our most important consideration.

1. Here is what our learner, Kathy, sees when she opens the quiz and clicks on the **Attempt quiz** button:

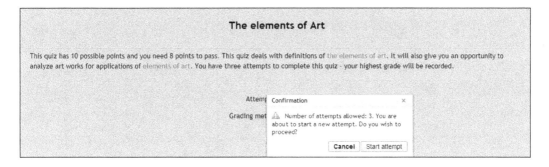

So she is informed of the number of attempts allowed and is given the opportunity to decide if she wants to proceed with this quiz now.

2. You can see that Kathy is provided with a navigation bar with her picture. It highlights the current question.

   Question number 1, the *Matching* question is the only question on page 1, as we had planned. Kathy has an option to flag a question to return to it later.

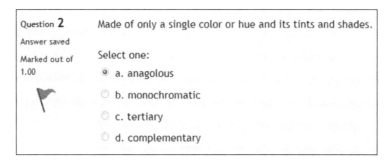

3. When Kathy clicks on **Next** at the end of the quiz or if she clicks on **End Test** in the navigation block, she is taken to **Summary of attempt**. This summary shows whether or not the question is answered and indicates any flagged questions. This is a good place for the learner to see if they have forgotten to answer any questions before they submit the quiz.

In the preceding screenshot, we can see that Kathy has flagged question 2, which she has not yet answered.

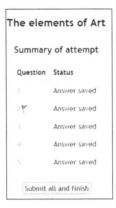

Now we can see that she has remembered to provide an answer for the flagged question before she submits the quiz.

4. When Kathy is sure that she has answered all questions, she can click on the **Submit all and finish** button to hand the quiz in for grading.

How it works...

Seeing how a test student proceeds through the quiz gives us insight into how the quiz is working with regard to the number of attempts, timelines, navigation, scoring, feedback, and flagged questions. If we notice any changes, we need to make that change before we open our quiz to our learners. We can delete the test student's attempt and make the desired changes.

Reviewing the quiz from the learner's perspective (Should know)

We can now review the graded quiz from the learner's perspective.

Getting ready

The learner has completed the quiz and it is graded. We can now see how our efforts and feedback decisions enhance the learning opportunities within our quiz.

How to do it...

Once the quiz is graded, Kathy can review it. If we have used no manual graded questions, the results are displayed immediately. If we have included a manual grade question, such as an essay question, that one will be displayed once it is graded.

1. The first indication of her quiz result is the overall data and results at the top of the page. Notice that she also receives the feedback that we planned at the whole quiz level.

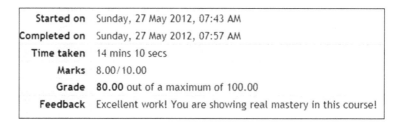

Started on	Sunday, 27 May 2012, 07:43 AM
Completed on	Sunday, 27 May 2012, 07:57 AM
Time taken	14 mins 10 secs
Marks	8.00 / 10.00
Grade	**80.00** out of a maximum of 100.00
Feedback	Excellent work! You are showing real mastery in this course!

2. Next, she can review **Quiz navigation** to see how she did in each question.

3. Each little box in the **Quiz navigation** block gives an indication of her results:
    - A correct response is colored green
    - An incorrect response is colored red
    - A partially correct multipart question would be colored yellow
    - A flagged question shows a mark in the top right corner

4. Question 2 that Kathy had flagged, was answered incorrectly, so it is colored red. If the question were answered correctly, the top right corner would still be marked to indicate the flag, but the box would be colored green. A more detailed review of each question is also provided.

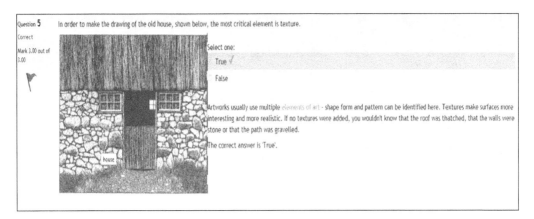

In this example, we can see the general feedback that we designed earlier for this *True or False* question.

5. This is what Kathy sees when she selects the quiz in her **Grades** view in the course:

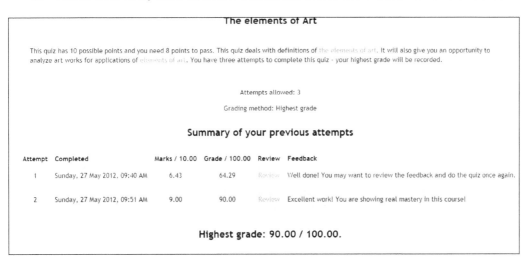

How it works...

Reviewing quiz results from our test student's perspective enables us to see how general and question level feedback will appear. We can then make necessary alterations before we decide to open the quiz to our learners.

The reviewing features of the quiz present additional learning opportunities. The instructor and learner can discuss specific content and understanding with a shared view of the learner's quiz results.

Quiz from the instructor's perspective (Should know)

In this recipe we will take a look at what the instructor sees once the learner has submitted the quiz. This allows the instructor to evaluate assessment choices (*for* and *of* learning), monitor learner progress, re-grade, and review class results.

Getting ready

The instructor can gain a great deal of useful information from the learner's completed quiz. The instructor can see all details of the completed quiz including flagged questions and gain some insight into any problems the student has faced. The instructor can also re-grade questions and add detailed personalized comments at the question level.

How to do it...

1. Go to **Settings | Course administration | Grades**:

2. In the drop down, click on **User report**:

3. On the far right of the screen, we choose the learner:

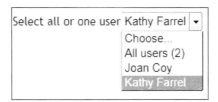

4. We choose the quiz we want to examine:

☑ The elements of Art	90.00	0-100	90.00 %

5. We have number of options in the **Preferences just for this page** area:

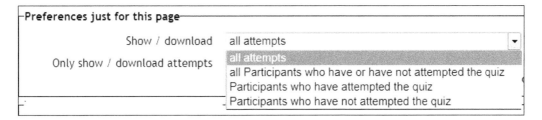

6. As an instructor, we are presented with a wealth of data for our learner on this quiz:

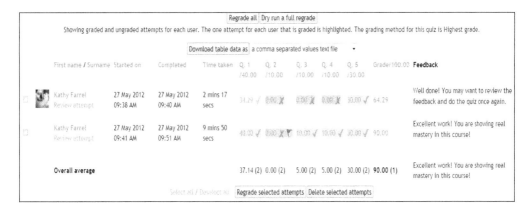

We can see the date and time for each attempt of the quiz and how long the learner spent doing it.

We can see details of each response.

- ❏ A correct response is colored green
- ❏ An incorrect response is colored red
- ❏ A partially correct multipart question is colored yellow
- ❏ A flagged question shows a mark in the top-right corner

We can see that the grade boundary comments that we created for this quiz are displayed for the learner.

We also have the ability to re-grade any item or delete a selected attempt of the quiz.

7. Let's drill down a little bit further with our learner Kathy's quiz. We notice that she has flagged question 2 in the second attempt. Click on the color-coded indicator for that question.

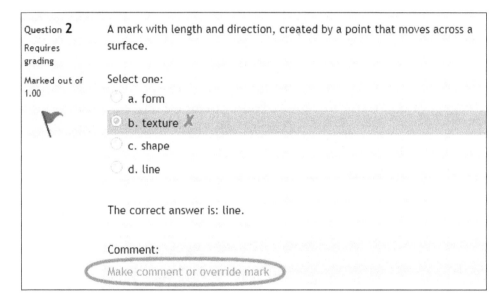

To comment or alter the grade of any question, the instructor needs to click on **Make comment or override mark**.

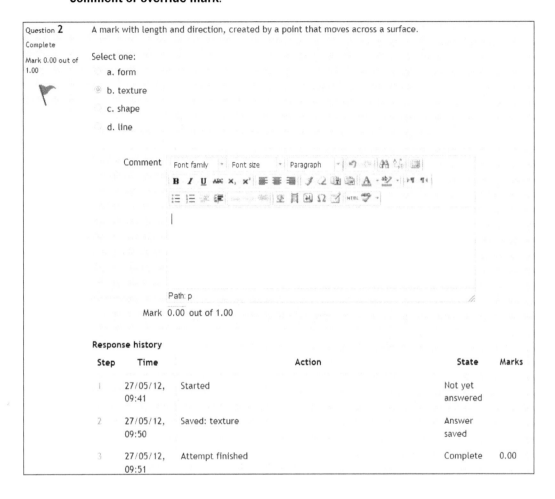

We can see the learner's choice and since Kathy has flagged this, we may learn more through a conversation with her. This is a great opportunity to clarify a concept or gain insight into improving a question. In this case, we followed up with a phone call.

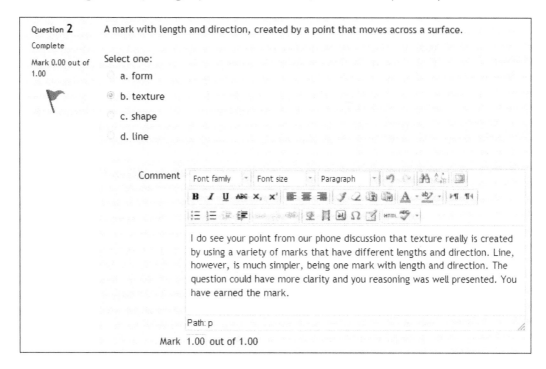

Remember that the purpose of this quiz is assessment *for* learning (formative) and the discussion generated is more important than the grade created.

Here is the report after our re-grading:

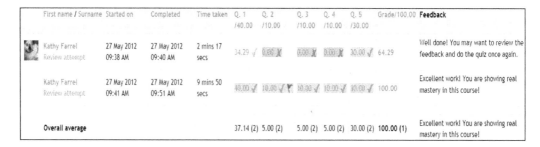

How it works...

Moodle Quiz provides the instructor with much detailed information using the learner's completed quiz. This includes overall score, number of attempts made, time spent on each attempt, performance on each item, and flagged questions. There is an opportunity for one-on-one interaction with the learner on specific questions to clarify the concepts.

We have seen how we can re-grade a particular question for a learner. If indeed the question needs to be revised, we can make the necessary changes in the question bank, and future attempts will use the revised question.

Quiz security (Should know)

Most often, instructors want to ensure that learners complete the quiz activities on their own. Quiz security is ensured through the Moodle Quiz settings and course design strategies.

Getting ready

Moodle Quiz is a very effective tool for creating tests and exams, and it is tempting to want to use it for high stakes exams that must be very secure. It is my opinion that this is not likely to be achievable in a web-based exam. If high security is required, consider providing in-person, supervised examinations.

When offering web-based exams, greater security is achieved through the Moodle Quiz settings and using course design strategies.

► Settings in Moodle Quiz to increase security:

These can be grouped into three categories.

   ❑ **Timelines**; We can restrict the period for which the quiz is open, create a time limit, restrict the number of attempts, and require a time delay between attempts.

   ❑ **User**: We can require a password and show the user's picture during the writing time.

   ❑ **Computer**: We can require a certain IP address and/or use a secure browser.

► Strategies in course design:

These can be grouped into two categories.

   ❑ **Quiz design**:

   Creates a very large question bank with many more questions than are needed and draws from these questions randomly so that no two quizzes are alike.

Shuffles both questions and choices within the questions in the quiz.

❏ **Alternate forms of assessment**:

Although Moodle Quiz is a powerful tool, it is best used in conjunction with other assessment measures. Effective course design will employ a number of performance-based assessments including projects, presentations, and portfolios.

How to do it...

In this section, we will discuss the settings available for the quiz security.

Settings in Moodle Quiz to increase the security

Quiz creators have a number of choices to increase the security.

▶ **Open the Quiz/Close the Quiz**: Restricting the period of time for which the quiz is open can reduce the chance of cheating. This quiz is now only open on one day.

▶ **Time limit**: A restricted time limit can be helpful in reducing the opportunity for the learner to consult external materials during the exam. Now, you can see that we have restricted the day on which the exam can be written and as well there is also a timer that begins when the student opens the exam. After 2 hours, the exam will close with only the answers submitted within the period of 2 hours.

▶ **Attempts allowed**: Restricting the attempts to only one attempt eliminates the chance to use the feedback information in future attempts.

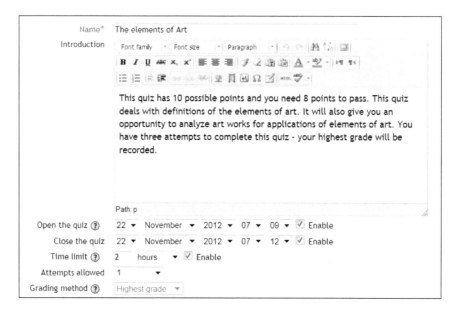

▶ **Shuffle within questions**: When we enable this setting, it means that parts of a question, such as multiple choices, will be randomly shuffled each time the quiz is displayed. This makes copying from a fellow learner difficult.

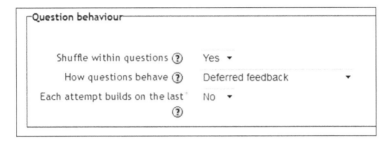

A large question bank affords greater flexibility to use random questions so that no two quizzes are alike.

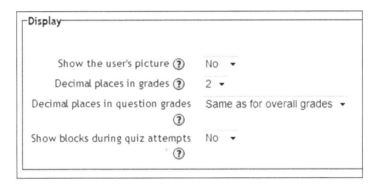

▶ **Show the user's picture**: If **Yes** is chosen here, the learner's profile photo will be displayed while that learner is taking the quiz. When actual students' photos are used for profiles, these can be used as identification during supervised examinations.

Of course, our system must be set to ensure the profile photo is the official one. Some learners use creative photos when self-enrolling! This is important to remember as Moodle is designed to allow students full editing access to their profiles.

Moodle quiz has an area of extra restrictions that is particularly useful when the instructor is concerned about secure quiz administration.

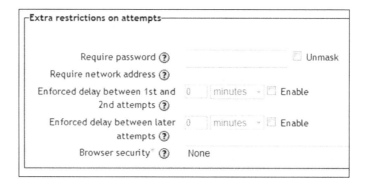

▶ **Require password**: We can require the student to enter a password in order to be able to take the quiz. When **Unmask** is checked, password will be shown—handy for the instructor, in case the password is forgotten.

▶ **Require network address**: The instructor has a number of options here, including specifying a single IP or an IP range. For example, if we enter 169.254.219.173, the learner can access the quiz only from that single computer. If this is our school, entering 169.254 would allow a range of IP addresses in our school, but nowhere else.

▶ **Enforced delay between 1st and 2nd attempts/Enforced delay between later attempts**: These two settings allow the instructor to determine a time delay between multiple quiz attempts. Of course, this applies only when the instructor has enabled multiple attempts for the quiz.

▶ **Browser security**: if the setting **Full screen pop-up with some Java-Script security** is used; the quiz is launched in a new window. Java-Script is used to disable copying, saving, and printing of the quiz.

Strategies in the course design

Performance assessment used in conjunction with tests provide a more complete assessment of student's learning and more accurate evaluation of higher-order thinking skills, such as analysis, synthesis, interpretation, and evaluation. Performance assessments challenge students to put their knowledge into context that can be understood and explained. When we use the Quiz tool in conjunction with performance assessment tools, we are able to provide both assessment *for* learning and assessment *of* learning that is comprehensive and respectful of learner differences.

Quiz reports (Become an expert)

Review and analysis of students' results is an important tool in improving instructions. We will examine the **Grades**, **Responses**, **Statistics**, and **Manual grading** reports.

Getting ready

- ▶ **Grades**: This report is essentially what we saw by going to **Grades | User report | Quiz**. It shows all the learners' quiz attempts, with the overall grade and the grade for each question. We can review all the details of a learner's attempt, seeing just what the student sees.

- ▶ **Responses**: This report allows the teacher to see a table of answers for a quiz, with a row for each learner.

- ▶ **Statistics**: This report is an analysis of the quiz and the questions within it.

   - ❑ The top section of this report gives a summary of the whole quiz.

   - ❑ The next section gives an analysis showing all questions in a table format. There are links in this section to drill down into a detailed analysis of a particular question.

   - ❑ The last section of this report is a bar graph representing the analysis of the quiz.

- ▶ **Manual grading**: This report lists all the questions in the quiz that need to be, or have been, manually graded (for example, essay questions) with the number of attempts.

How to do it...

As instructors, we find it very useful to analyze the quizzes we have given. This provides an opportunity to improve both the quizzes and the instruction. There are a number of reports that are available to the instructor for each quiz in Moodle 2.2, which allow us to see details of each response given by all students. To access the reports:

1. Go to the **Navigation** block.

2. Go to the relevant course—in this case **PAVE Art** and to the quiz we are interested in—in this case **The elements of Art**.

3. Click on **Results** and you will see the four report types, **Grades**, **Responses**, **Statistics**, or **Manual grading** revealed.

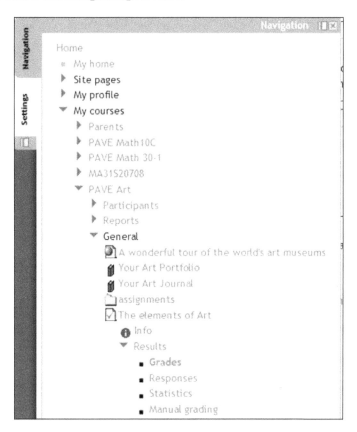

Let's take a closer look at each of these reports.

The Grades report

When we click on this report, we see the preferences area where we can customize the report.

▸ **Preferences just for this page**: This area allows us to control what is displayed.

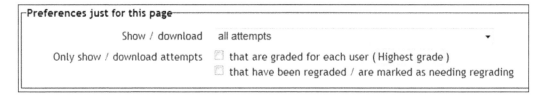

This area allows us to show all attempts, learners who have attempted the quiz, or learners who have not attempted the quiz. This is handy for monitoring students' progress in the course.

▶ **Your preferences for this report**: Here you can choose the degree of detail you want the report to show.

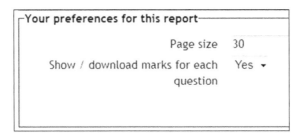

▶ **Report**: The report itself gives us a wealth of information.

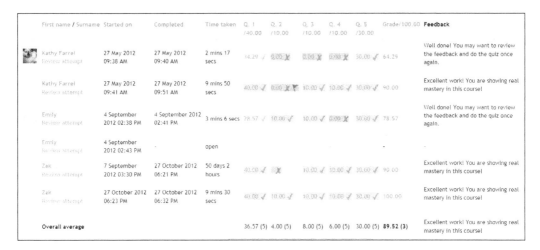

Under the student name, when we click on **Review attempt**, we see the actual graded student quiz. The report gives the date and time taken to complete the quiz by each learner. It then gives a breakdown question-by-question indicating:

- ❏ Green highlight for correct responses
- ❏ Red highlight for incorrect responses
- ❏ Yellow highlight for partially correct responses

It also shows any questions students have flagged.

Overall feedback on the quiz provided to the learner is also shown.

You have a number of choices to decide how you can download this report.

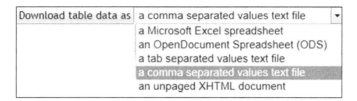

At the bottom of the page, a graph shows the distribution of scores. This one represents the work of three test students. It is much more informative with data from a whole class.

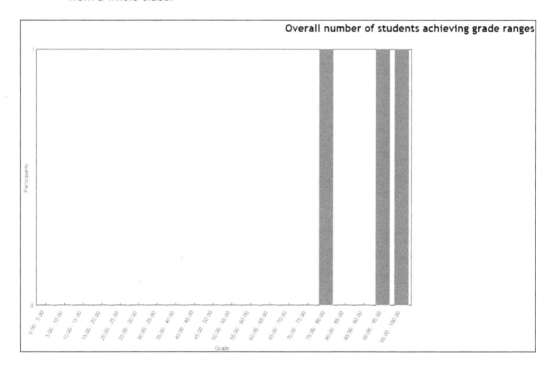

You can select individual attempts by clicking in the checkbox on the left of the table, or choose **Select all/Deselect all** to select/deselect all attempts by using the options underneath the table, and then re-grade or delete the selected attempts.

The Responses report

This shows the answers given by each student for each question, highlighting whether they are correct or not, but it does not show the students' scores.

▶ **Preferences just for this page**: Again, you can control what you see on the report by setting preferences at the top of the page, you can delete attempts, and you can download the information in a variety of formats.

┌─**Preferences just for this page**──

Show / download	all attempts ▾
Only show / download attempts	☐ that are graded for each user (Highest grade)
Include	☐ Summary of the question
	☑ Summary of the response given
	☐ Summary of the right answer

Once again we can show all attempts, learners who have attempted the quiz, or learners who have not attempted the quiz.

The **Preferences just for this page** section has **Summary of the response given** selected by default. You may choose to deselect this or to include a summary of the question and the right answer, if you prefer.

▶ **Report**: The report is shown in the following screenshot:

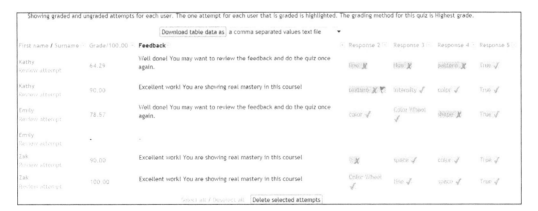

The Statistics report

This report provides statistical analysis of the quiz, such as average grades and distribution of scores.

▶ **Quiz information**: The **Quiz information** report is shown in the following screenshot:

	Quiz information
	Download full report as a comma separated values text file ▼
Quiz name	The elements of Art
Course name	PAVE Art
Number of complete graded first attempts	3
Total number of complete graded attempts	5
Average grade of first attempts	77.62%
Average grade of all attempts	84.57%
Median grade (for all attempts)	90.00%
Standard deviation (for all attempts)	13.64%

▶ **Quiz structure analysis**: The **Quiz structure analysis** table is shown in the following screenshot:

Quiz structure analysis

Download table data as a comma separated values text file ▼

Q#			Question name	Attempts	Facility index	Standard deviation	Random guess score	Intended weight	Effective weight	Discrimination index	Discriminative efficiency
1			Elements of Art	5	91.43%	12.78%	14.29%	40.00%	25.27%	35.72%	41.18%
2			Random (Elements of Art Definitions and sub-categories)	5	40.00%	54.77%		10.00%	18.07%	-9.03%	-13.64%
3			Random (Elements of Art Definitions and sub-categories)	5	80.00%	44.72%		10.00%	26.50%	67.12%	100.00%
4			Random (Elements of Art Definitions and sub-categories)	5	60.00%	54.77%		10.00%	30.16%	70.85%	100.00%
			line	2	50.00%	70.71%	25.00%	10.00%		100.00%	100.00%
			space	2	100.00%	0.00%	25.00%	10.00%			
			form	1	0.00%	0.00%	25.00%	10.00%			
			color	1	100.00%	0.00%	25.00%	10.00%			
			shape	1	0.00%		25.00%	10.00%			
			color wheel	2	100.00%	0.00%	25.00%	10.00%			
			intensity	2	50.00%	70.71%	25.00%	10.00%		100.00%	100.00%
5			Application of the element Texture	5	100.00%	0.00%	50.00%	30.00%	0.00%		

The **Quiz structure analysis** section gives a good variety of information about the quiz that allows us to identify our best questions and gives us the opportunity to remove or revise poorly performing questions.

- First of all, it shows the number of attempts made on the quiz—an important factor before we begin to draw conclusions from the statistical information.

- **Facility index** is basically a measure of how easy or difficult a question is for a learner.

- **Standard deviation** is a measure of the spread of responses in the population of learners. For example, a value of zero on a question would indicate that every learner gave the same response.

- **Random guess score** is an estimate of the score a student could achieve by guessing alone.

- **Intended weight** is the relative amount that each question will count towards the final score.

- **Effective weight** is an estimate from the results—how much variation is caused by a particular question.

- **Discrimination index** is an indicator of the performance of a question to separate high and low scorers on the quiz. This measure uses the top third of the scores and the bottom third of the scores for the calculation.

- **Discrimination efficiency** is also a measure of the power of the question to distinguish between high and low scorers. This measure is a correlation coefficient between scores for the question and the whole quiz.

  For both **Discrimination index** and **Discrimination efficiency**, the score can be between −1 and +1. Positive values indicate questions that do discriminate proficient learners, indicating that higher scorers tended to select the correct option. Negative values indicate questions that are answered best by those with lowest grades, not really what we intend!

❑ This report not only provides statistical analysis of the quiz, but also allows us to drill down into individual questions for detailed analysis. You can download the **Quiz information** report and the **Quiz structure analysis** table in various formats.

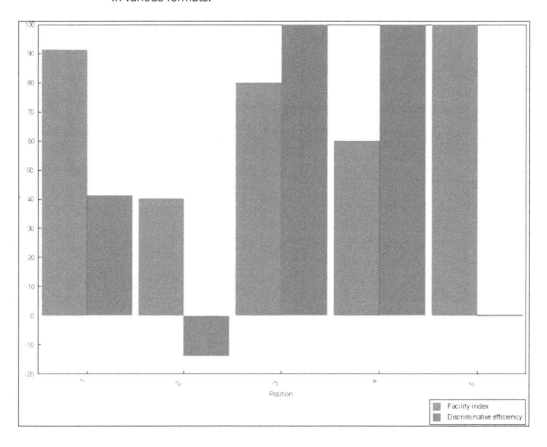

For more detailed information on the **Statistics** report, go to `http://docs.moodle.org/22/en/Quiz_statistics_report`.

The Manual grading report

This report concerns the questions that need manual grading, such as Essay questions. It is a good location to grade or re-grade this form of question.

We can click on the **Also show questions that have been graded automatically** link to edit all grades.

For more information on the **Manual grading** report, go to `http://docs.moodle.org/22/en/Quiz_manual_grading_report`.

How it works...

In Moodle 2.0, more graphs and visual representations have been added to give us a quick overview. The **Responses** report allows the download of all learners' answers, so the question performance can be examined. The **Statistics** report provides very detailed information and the tools we need as instructors to improve the instructions.

There's more...

For on-going shared information from the instructors using Moodle Quiz, the *Frequently Asked Questions* site is really helpful (`http://docs.moodle.org/21/en/Quiz_FAQ`).

Thank you for buying
**Instant Moodle Quiz Module
How-to**

About Packt Publishing

Packt, pronounced 'packed', published its first book "*Mastering phpMyAdmin for Effective MySQL Management*" in April 2004 and subsequently continued to specialize in publishing highly focused books on specific technologies and solutions.

Our books and publications share the experiences of your fellow IT professionals in adapting and customizing today's systems, applications, and frameworks. Our solution based books give you the knowledge and power to customize the software and technologies you're using to get the job done. Packt books are more specific and less general than the IT books you have seen in the past. Our unique business model allows us to bring you more focused information, giving you more of what you need to know, and less of what you don't.

Packt is a modern, yet unique publishing company, which focuses on producing quality, cutting-edge books for communities of developers, administrators, and newbies alike. For more information, please visit our website: www.packtpub.com.

Writing for Packt

We welcome all inquiries from people who are interested in authoring. Book proposals should be sent to author@packtpub.com. If your book idea is still at an early stage and you would like to discuss it first before writing a formal book proposal, contact us; one of our commissioning editors will get in touch with you.

We're not just looking for published authors; if you have strong technical skills but no writing experience, our experienced editors can help you develop a writing career, or simply get some additional reward for your expertise.

Moodle Gradebook

ISBN: 978-1-849518-14-7   Paperback: 128 pages

Set up and customize the gradebook to track student progress through Moodle

1. Use Moodle's powerful gradebook more effectively to monitor and report on the progress of your students

2. Customize the gradebook to calculate and show the information you need

3. Discover new grading features and tracking functions now available in Moodle 2

Moodle 2 for Teaching 7-14 Year Olds Beginner's Guide

ISBN: 978-1-849518-32-1   Paperback: 258 pages

Effective e-learning for younger students, using Moodle as your classroom assistant

1. Ideal for teachers new to Moodle: easy to follow and abundantly illustrated with screenshots of the solutions you'll build

2. Go paperless! Put your lessons online and grade them anywhere, anytime

3. Engage and motivate your students with games, quizzes, movies, blogs and podcasts the whole class can participate in

Please check **www.PacktPub.com** for information on our titles

www.ingramcontent.com/pod-product-compliance
Lightning Source LLC
LaVergne TN
LVHW080103070326
832902LV00014B/2399